Cornelia Funke

My Favorite Writer

Tatiana Tomljanovic

WEIGL PUBLISHERS INC.

Published by Weigl Publishers Inc.
350 5th Avenue, Suite 3304, PMB 6G
New York, NY   10118-0069

Web site: www.weigl.com

Library of Congress Cataloging-in-Publication Data

Tomljanovic, Tatiana.
  Cornelia Funke : my favorite writer / Tatiana Tomljanovic.
     p. cm. -- (My favorite writer)
  Includes index.
  ISBN 1-59036-480-5 (library binding : alk. paper) -- ISBN 1-59036-
481-3 (soft cover : alk. paper)
  1. Funke, Cornelia Caroline--Juvenile literature. 2. Authors, German--
20th century--Biography--Juvenile literature. 3. Children's stories--
Authorship--Juvenile literature. I. Title. II. Series.
  PT2666.U49Z85 2007
  833'.914--dc22
  [B]
                                                    2006015265

Printed in the United States of America
1 2 3 4 5 6 7 8 9 0 09 08 07 06 05

All of the Internet URLs given in the book were valid at the time of
publication. However, due to the dynamic nature of the Internet, some
addresses may have changed, or sites may have ceased to exist since
publication. While the author and publisher regret any inconvenience this
may cause readers, no responsibility for any such changes can be accepted
by either the author or the publisher.

Project Coordinator
Heather C. Hudak

Design
Terry Paulhus

Contents

Cornelia Funke

MILESTONES

1958 Born December 10 in Dorsten, Germany

1976 Moves to Hamburg to attend college

1986 Begins writing books

1989 Daughter, Anna, is born on December 10

1994 Son, Ben, is born on November 14

2000 Wins Zurich Children's Book Award for *The Thief Lord*

2002 An English version of *The Thief Lord* is published

2005 Family moves from Hamburg, Germany, to Los Angeles, California

Cornelia Funke creates fantastic worlds filled with dragons, magic, and heroes. She is the third most popular author in Germany, the country where she was born. Cornelia's books are quickly becoming popular throughout Europe and North America.

At first, Cornelia became an **illustrator** of children's books. Eventually, she began to write her own stories.

Cornelia has written more than 40 books. She writes her books in German. Her first book, *The Thief Lord,* was translated into English. It became a *New York Times* best-seller. *The Thief Lord* is about two orphaned brothers, Prosper and Bo. After their mother's death, they move in with their mean aunt. In order to escape, the boys run away to Venice. In Venice, the brothers join a gang of young thieves. The gang is led by the mysterious Thief Lord.

Cornelia's books are set in real places, such as Venice, but they are full of magic and **fantasy**. Her stories are meant to spark the imagination of young readers.

Early Childhood

Cornelia Caroline Funke was born on December 10, 1958, in Dorsten, a small city in Germany. She is the oldest of four children. Cornelia's brother Volker is two years younger than Cornelia. Their brother Elmar was born four years after Volker. Their sister, Insa, was born when Cornelia was 14 years old.

■ The city of Dorsten lies on the Lippe River and the Wesel-Dateln Canal in western Germany. Fewer than 100,000 people live there.

NETHERLANDS

GERMANY

Amsterdam

62°

★ **Dorsten**

Brussels

BELGIUM

LUX.
Luxembourg

N
W—E
S

0   50   100 Kilometers

0   50   100 Miles

Cornelia's parents, Helmi and Karl Heinz Funke, had a good sense of humor. They were patient and kind with their children. Karl was a **bookworm**. Karl took Cornelia and her younger siblings to the library every Saturday. Cornelia's grandmother was good at telling stories. Cornelia loved to listen to her tales. Cornelia's love of reading came from her father and grandmother.

Cornelia's grandfather was a well-known etcher in Germany. An etcher is an artist who cuts designs or pictures onto metal using a sharp tool or an acid.

■ Germany is known for its hundreds of medieval castles.

Growing Up

As a child, Cornelia never thought of being a writer. She wanted to be an astronaut. When she grew older, she learned that she would have to train with the **military** to become an astronaut. Cornelia did not want military training, so she gave up the idea of being an astronaut. Later, Cornelia wanted to be a pilot or marry a Native American chief and live with his family. She was very serious about these plans, although she never became any of those things.

Growing up, Cornelia not only loved to read, she also liked to watch movies and attend games at the soccer stadium. Cornelia liked watching soccer games, but she did not enjoy playing sports in school. To this day, Cornelia does not like playing sports. For exercise, she prefers to take a long walk with her dog, Luna.

Cornelia attended St. Ursula Gymnasium School in Dorsten. Her favorite subjects in school were German and English. She loved books and writing essays.

Soccer is a popular sport in Hamburg, Germany.

Although Cornelia did well in school, she was not very **ambitious**. She even describes herself as lazy in school. However, Cornelia did like to write essays. She wrote longer essays than her teachers wanted, and she rarely stayed on the topic her teachers assigned.

After high school, Cornelia left Dorsten. She studied education at the University of Hamburg. She wanted to work with children.

When she graduated, Cornelia became a social worker. A social worker is a person who works with people in a **community** who need help, such as children or families who are poor or have special needs. After three years, Cornelia realized she was better at drawing than at being a social worker. She decided to return to school.

Inspired to Write

Cornelia sets her stories in real places. For instance, *The Thief Lord* takes place in Venice. Cornelia wants her characters to be in places that children can visit.

At St. Ursula, Cornelia's favorite teacher was her German teacher. He encouraged Cornelia's love of literature.

Cornelia studied illustration at the *Hochschule für Angewandte Wissenschaften* (HAW) in the Faculty of Design, Media, and Information. After finishing a course at HAW, she became a children's book illustrator.

Over time, Cornelia became disappointed with the kinds of books she was asked to illustrate. When Cornelia worked with children as a social worker, she discovered that they enjoyed stories about amazing creatures and exciting adventures. These were also the kinds of stories Cornelia enjoyed reading. She wanted to draw fantastic characters and situations, not everyday events. She decided to write and illustrate her own stories.

■ Cornelia attended college in Hamburg, Germany.

"Most adults will want to make you believe that by 18 at the latest you should have figured out what kind of profession is the right one for you. Don't believe a word of that!"
Cornelia Funke

The legends of King Arthur are some of Cornelia's favorite stories.

Favorite Authors

When Cornelia was growing up, her favorite book was *The Once and Future King* by T.H. White. It is a story about Arthur and the Knights of the Round Table. Cornelia loved Arthurian **legends**. Some of her other favorite books were *Tom Sawyer, The Chronicles of Narnia,* a German book called *Jim Button,* and *Lucas the Steam Engine Driver*.

Learning the Craft

Cornelia loves to read and write fantasy stories. She loves writing fantasy because it does not limit her imagination.

Cornelia did not begin writing until she was 28 years old. She never had any formal training. She did take a college illustration course that helps her draw the characters in her stories. Cornelia draws her characters before she writes about them. This helps her to see the characters more clearly and imagine where they might go and what they might enjoy.

Cornelia learned her craft by reading. She has loved reading since she was a young girl. Every week, Cornelia would visit the library and choose all kinds of books to read—not just fantasy novels. She read different **genres**, such as fantasy, horror, comedy, romance, action, and nonfiction. Cornelia learned about different types of stories and styles of writing. She also learned what makes a good story—interesting and believable characters, an entertaining plot, and well-written sentences. She applied what she learned to her writing.

J. M. Barrie's story of Peter Pan has inspired Cornelia.

Cornelia soon realized she loved writing even more than she loved drawing. She began writing every day. Cornelia has been writing every day for the last 20 years. After years of practice, Cornelia's writing has improved. She says that her best works are *Inkheart* and *Inkspell,* her most recent novels. She is very proud of these books. Of all the books she has written so far, these are her favorite stories.

Cornelia **quotes** lines from other well-known books at the beginning of every chapter in *Inkheart.* Some of the books she quotes are *Peter Pan, Treasure Island, The Sword In the Stone,* and *The Princess Bride.* They are all **classic** children's stories.

Inspired to Write

Cornelia wrote *Dragon Rider* because she has always wanted to ride a dragon. After she wrote the story, Cornelia learned that the dragon she drew for the book looked exactly like her editor's dog.

The Princess Bride tells the story of a beautiful young princess and her true love. It was made into a movie in 1987.

Getting Published

Barry Cunningham helped open up Cornelia's books to English-speaking readers.

Cornelia didn't become a full-time writer until she was 35 years old. However, she quickly became one of the most popular children's authors in Germany. No publisher has ever turned down the chance to publish one of Cornelia's books.

Despite Cornelia's success in Germany, the rest of the world did not know who she was until recently. One of Cornelia's fans, a young girl who could read both German and English, wrote a letter to a British publisher named Barry Cunningham. The girl asked Barry why there were no books in English by her favorite writer, Cornelia Funke. Barry became curious about Cornelia's books. He tracked down one of her titles, *Herr der Diebe*—the German title of *The Thief Lord*. Barry liked the book so much that he helped publish it in English in 2002. The story was **translated** from German into English by Cornelia's cousin.

The Publishing Process

Publishing companies receive hundreds of **manuscripts** from authors each year. Only a few manuscripts become books. Publishers must be sure that a manuscript will sell many copies. As a result, publishers reject most of the manuscripts they receive.

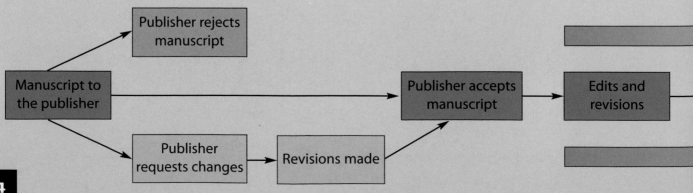

The Thief Lord has won several **international** awards, including The Mildred L. Batchelder Award for the best translated children's book. Since then, several of Cornelia's books have been translated into English. One of them is *Inkheart*, the first novel in a three-part series. *Inkheart* has been popular with both fans and **critics**.

Cornelia always writes her stories in German. However, she knows English very well. She reads and approves all English translations of her books before they are published.

Some of Cornelia's books have been so popular that they have been made into movies. *The Thief Lord* was released as a movie in 2005. *Inkheart* is also being made into a movie.

When Cornelia wrote *Inkheart,* she imagined the character Mo as Brendan Fraser, the Hollywood actor. After Cornelia wrote the book, she and Brendan met and became friends. Brendan recorded an **audio** version of another one of Cornelia's books, called *Dragon Rider*.

Inspired to Write

Cornelia sometimes bases her characters on people she knows or sees on TV and in movies. Bo in *The Thief Lord* is a little bit like her son, Ben, when he was little. Victor, another character from *The Thief Lord*, is similar to the British actor Bob Hoskins. Mo from *Inkheart* reminds Cornelia of the actor Brendan Fraser.

"I will try to write books until I drop dead."
Cornelia Funke

Once a manuscript has been accepted, it goes through many stages before it is published. Often, authors change their work to follow an editor's suggestions. Once the book is published, some authors receive royalties. This is money based on book sales.

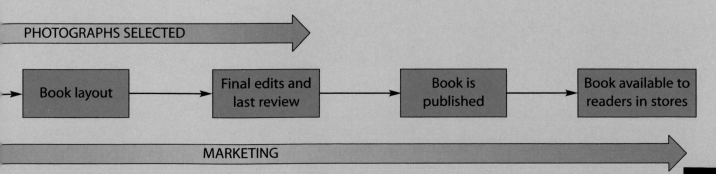

PHOTOGRAPHS SELECTED

Book layout → Final edits and last review → Book is published → Book available to readers in stores

MARKETING

Writer Today

Cornelia lives in Los Angeles, California, with her children, Anna and Ben. Cornelia's husband of 26 years, Rolf, died of cancer in March 2006. Even when he was in the hospital being treated for cancer, Rolf asked Cornelia to bring her notebook with her every day. He wanted her to continue to write while keeping him company.

Cornelia knows Rolf would want her to keep writing. One of her favorite places to write is at a little table in a small house in Malibu, California. Cornelia can hear the Pacific Ocean from inside the house. Cornelia also spends time in Hamburg, Germany. She has a special writing room in Hamburg. It is filled with a stuffed dragon collection and gifts that fans have sent.

■ The coast of Malibu, California, inspires Cornelia to write.

Cornelia and her family have many pets. They own two Icelandic ponies named Snegla and Jarpur. In Icelandic, Snegla means "woman with the expressive face" and Jarpur means "the brown one." The Funkes also have a shy guinea pig and a big shaggy dog named Luna.

Cornelia likes to spend time with her family, so she rises early in the morning to write. Sometimes she rewrites in the evening. She often writes into the middle of the night in order to meet her deadlines.

Cornelia keeps busy **promoting** her books. Members of her family help her in any way they can. Cornelia's brother is her lawyer. Her sister answers Cornelia's fan mail. Cornelia's cousin serves as her manager. Before he died, Rolf gave up his job as a printer to help Cornelia with her career. Their children, Anna and Ben, are first to read Cornelia's books. They tell her what they like, what they do not like, and what they think she should change.

■ Cornelia's family nicknamed their dog Looney because of his crazy behavior. Looney likes to chew on Cornelia's stuffed penguin.

Popular Books

Cornelia Funke loves to write for children. She has earned many honors for her work, including several awards in Germany. Some of her children's novels are so popular that both adults and children read them. Following are some of her most popular books.

Dragon Rider

Dragon Rider is a 500-page novel about Firedrake, a young silver dragon. Firedrake learns that people are about to discover the valley where the silver dragons live. He decides to find the Rim of Heaven, a magical place in the Himalayas where silver dragons can live in peace. Ben, an orphaned boy, and Sorrell, a grumpy Scottish **brownie**, go with Firedrake on his journey. Ben and Sorrell ride on Firedrake's back as he flies around the world in search of the Rim of Heaven. The three travelers encounter many dangers, including Nettlebrand, an evil creature covered in gold plates. Nettlebrand wants to destroy all of the silver dragons. Firedrake, Ben, and Sorrell outwit Nettlebrand and have many adventures. They also make friends with different people and creatures along the way.

The Thief Lord

The Thief Lord is a story about how much children can care for one another—even in the worst **circumstances**. *The Thief Lord* has won many awards in the United States, Germany, and around the world.

  The story is about two brothers, Prosper, age 12, and Bo, age 5. After their mother dies, their aunt, Esther Hartlieb, wants to adopt Bo but not Prosper. The brothers refuse to be separated. They run away together to Venice, a city their mother loved. The boys begin living in an abandoned movie theater with a gang of young thieves led by the Thief Lord. The Thief Lord is a masked boy named Scipio. He steals from rich **Venetians** to provide food and clothes for his friends. The gang members' lives are turned upside down when Scipio tries to steal a broken wooden wing that completes a magical merry-go-round. The merry-go-round can turn children into adults and adults into children.

AWARDS
The Thief Lord

2002 *New York Times* Notable Book Of The Year

2003 Torchlight Children's Book Award

2003 Book Sense Book of the Year, Children's Literature

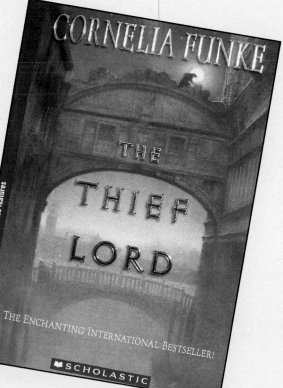

CORNELIA FUNKE

THE THIEF LORD

Includes AFTER WORDS™ bonus features

THE ENCHANTING INTERNATIONAL BESTSELLER!

SCHOLASTIC

Inkheart

Inkheart is the first book in a three-part series about Mo, a book binder, and Meggie, his daughter. Mo has an amazing but dangerous ability. When he reads aloud from a book, he brings the characters to life. Every time Mo reads and brings a character out of a book, someone from the real world must take his or her place in the book world. When Meggie was 3, Mo read the book *Inkheart*. He accidentally brought the story's villain, Capricorn, to life. This caused Meggie's mother to be sent into the book.

Mo hides his powerful ability from Meggie for years. Meggie, now 12, only knows that Mo refuses to read to her. She learns more when Dustfinger, one of the characters Mo reads to life, warns Mo that Capricorn is searching for him. Capricorn wants to use Mo's ability for evil. Soon Mo and Meggie are pulled into the world of Inkheart and must fight to stay alive.

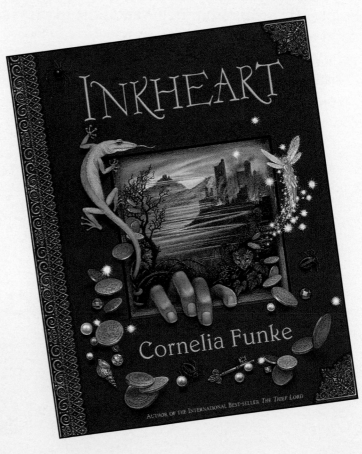

The Princess Knight

The Princess Knight is a funny story with many pictures. In *The Princess Knight*, King Wilfred the Worthy has three sons and one daughter. His daughter's name is Violetta. Unlike most princesses, Violetta does not learn to sew or play music. She learns how to be a knight. Violetta learns how to ride a horse, **joust**, fight with a sword, and shout very loudly. When Violetta's father announces that she must marry the winner of a jousting competition, Violetta tricks everyone and wins the competition.

Pirate Girl

Pirate Girl is another funny story with colorful pictures. Captain Firebeard and his band of pirates **terrorize** peaceful sailors. Aboard their ship, *Horrible Haddock*, they travel and steal from people on other ships. One day, they capture young Molly and her ship. The pirates are mean to Molly. They make her clean their ship and peel potatoes. Molly does not have to peel potatoes for long. Her mother, Barbarous Bertha, a pirate who is even scarier than Captain Firebeard, rescues Molly. Barbarous Bertha then makes Captain Firebeard and his crew clean her ship.

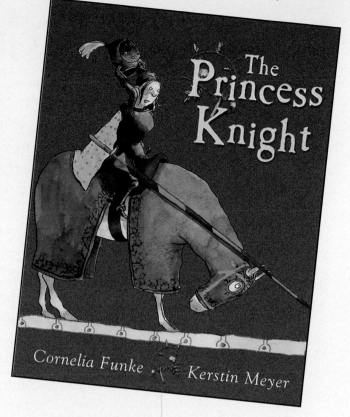

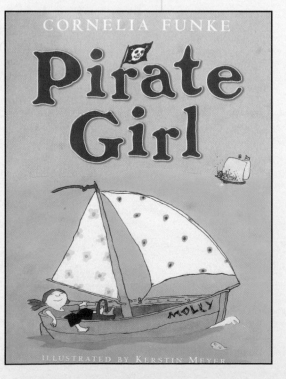

Creative Writing Tips

"Revision makes writing sparkle, makes it dense and beautiful."
Cornelia Funke

Writers work hard to come up with good ideas. They have to work even harder to put those ideas into words that entertain readers. The following are some tips that help Cornelia write her books.

Read

Most writers, including Cornelia Funke, read a great deal. Exploring different books, subjects, and styles of writing helps authors improve their writing. Reading helps build vocabulary and improve sentence structure. It also exposes writers to different subjects and styles. Then, writers can develop their own style of writing from what they have learned from others.

Research

Even when writing fiction, research is a very important part of creating good stories. Carefully researched stories have a high level of detail that creates a more believable tale. Cornelia takes time to research all of her novels. Before writing *Inkheart*, she studied booksellers, book collectors, and book thieves. She also researched **martens** and fire eaters.

Cornelia's advice to anyone who would like to become an author is to "read, read, read."

Plan

Each story, novel, or piece of writing must have a structure. It should have a beginning, middle, and end. These parts make books understandable to readers. Once a writer has an idea for a story and has researched the details that will be included, he or she must plan how to tell the story. Cornelia likes to imagine her characters and the places they might visit. She writes down plot lines for the first 20 chapters. Only after she has done all of this does she write the first sentence.

Rewrite

It often takes many tries to get something right. Writing is no different. Authors will rewrite stories several times before they are complete. Grammar needs to be corrected, spelling checked, details changed, and sentences reworded. Cornelia usually writes three or four drafts of a story before she hands it to her publisher. She also reads the whole story out loud to herself to make sure it sounds right. A novel takes Cornelia more than a year to write.

Inspired to Write

Cornelia comes up with the unusual names for the characters in her books by looking up the names of animals and plants in encyclopedias. For *Inkheart* and *The Thief Lord*, she looked in Italian dictionaries, Italian history books, and at lists of Italian names.

■ Do not be afraid to make mistakes when you write.

Writing a Biography Review

A biography is an account of an individual's life that is written by another person. Some people's lives are very interesting. In school, you may be asked to write a biography review. The first thing to do when writing a biography review is to decide whom you would like to learn about. Your school library or community library will have a large selection of biographies from which to choose.

Are you interested in an author, a sports figure, an inventor, a movie star, or a president? Finding the right book is your first task. Whether you choose to write your review on a biography of Cornelia Funke or another person, the task will be similar.

Begin your review by writing the title of the book, the author, and the person featured in the book. Then, start writing about the main events in the person's life. Include such things as where the person grew up and what his or her childhood was like. You will want to add details about the person's adult life, such as whether he or she married or had children. Next, write about what you think makes this person special. What kinds of experiences influenced this individual? For instance, did he or she grow up in unusual circumstances? Was the person determined to accomplish a goal? Include any details that surprised you.

A concept web is a useful research tool. Use the concept web on the right to begin researching your biography review.

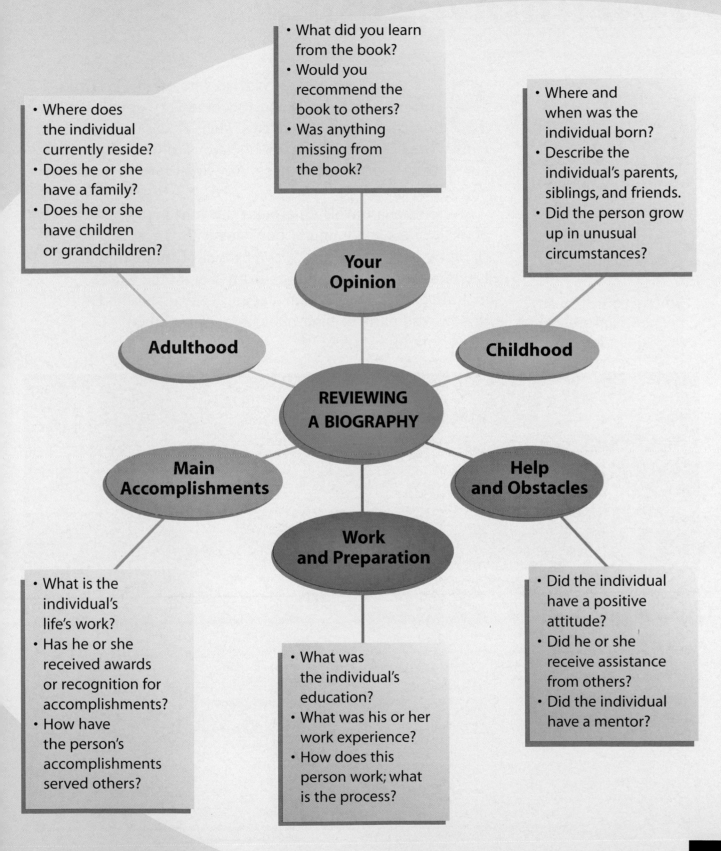

- Where does the individual currently reside?
- Does he or she have a family?
- Does he or she have children or grandchildren?

- What did you learn from the book?
- Would you recommend the book to others?
- Was anything missing from the book?

- Where and when was the individual born?
- Describe the individual's parents, siblings, and friends.
- Did the person grow up in unusual circumstances?

Your Opinion

Adulthood

Childhood

REVIEWING A BIOGRAPHY

Main Accomplishments

Help and Obstacles

Work and Preparation

- What is the individual's life's work?
- Has he or she received awards or recognition for accomplishments?
- How have the person's accomplishments served others?

- What was the individual's education?
- What was his or her work experience?
- How does this person work; what is the process?

- Did the individual have a positive attitude?
- Did he or she receive assistance from others?
- Did the individual have a mentor?

Fan Information

Cornelia has written two new books that have been translated in English. They are *The Wildest Brother* and *Ghosthunters and the Incredibly Revolting Ghost!*

■ Like Cornelia, many people enjoy spending time in the library.

Since the release of the English version of *The Thief Lord,* Cornelia Funke has become very popular in English-speaking countries, such as the United States. Fans write her letters and post questions to Cornelia on her website. Cornelia also has many loyal fans in her native Germany.

Cornelia travels all around the world reading her books to fans and going to book festivals. In April 2005, she took part in the New York Festival of International Literature. Children's authors from around the world, including Germany, Britain, Japan, Kenya, and the United States, read parts of their books and shared their ideas with one another.

If you want to know more about Cornelia and her books, visit her website. It lists all of her books and awards in both German and English. It also has many fun facts about Cornelia, such as her favorite things, and a message board for those who want to ask Cornelia questions.

■ Cornelia loves to take walks along the beach near Malibu, California.

WEB LINKS

Cornelia Funke's Website

www.corneliafunke.de/en

This is Cornelia's personal website. She talks about her writing, her opinions, and her family.

Publisher's Fan Website for Cornelia Funke

www.corneliafunkefans.com

This website provides information about movies based on Cornelia's books, reading guides and questions, and a list of stories by other authors about children in fantastic **circumstances**.

Quiz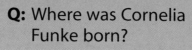

Q: Where was Cornelia Funke born?

1

A: Dorsten, Germany

Q: Who first published Cornelia's books in English?

2

A: Barry Cunningham

3

Q: Name one of Cornelia's books.

A: The Thief Lord, Inkheart, Dragon Rider, Pirate Girl, Inkspell, or The Princess Knight

The captivating sequel to *Inkheart*, the critically acclaimed international bestseller

INKSPELL

CORNELIA FUNKE

AUTHOR OF THE THIEF LORD AND DRAGON RIDER

4

Q: From which university did Cornelia graduate?

A: The University of Hamburg

5

Q: Where do Cornelia and her family live today?

A: Los Angeles, California

6

Q: What are Cornelia's children's names?

A: Anna and Ben

7

Q: What is Cornelia's favorite book?

A: *The Once and Future King* by T. H. White

8

Q: What is Mo's special skill in *Inkheart*?

A: He can bring characters to life by reading books out loud.

9

Q: When was Cornelia's first English book published?

A: 2002

10

Q: What were Cornelia's favorite subjects in school?

A: English and German

Writing Terms

This glossary will introduce you to some of the main terms in the field of writing. Understanding these common writing terms will allow you to discuss your ideas about books and writing with others.

action: the moving events of a work of fiction

antagonist: the person in the story who opposes the main character

autobiography: a history of a person's life written by that person

biography: a written account of another person's life

character: a person in a story, poem, or play

climax: the most exciting moment or turning point in a story

episode: a short piece of action, or scene, in a story

fiction: stories about characters and events that are not real

foreshadow: hinting at something that is going to happen later in the book

imagery: a written description of a thing or idea that brings an image to mind

narrator: the speaker of the story who relates the events

nonfiction: writing that deals with real people and events

novel: published writing of considerable length that portrays characters within a story

plot: the order of events in a work of fiction

protagonist: the leading character of a story; often a likable character

resolution: the end of the story, when the conflict is settled

scene: a single episode in a story

setting: the place and time in which a work of fiction occurs

theme: an idea that runs throughout a work of fiction

Glossary

ambitious: a strong desire to succeed

audio: something you can hear, such as a CD

bookworm: someone who loves to read

brownie: a fictional creature similar to a fairy

circumstances: state of events

classic: something that has stood the test of time

community: a group of people living in the same area

critics: people who offer their opinions

fantasy: something imagined that is not likely to happen in real life

genres: categories or types of stories

illustrator: someone who draws pictures

international: all around the world

joust: a medieval sport in which two knights try to knock each other off of horses with large sticks called lances

legends: old myths or stories

manuscripts: drafts of a story before it is published

martens: weasel-like animals

military: to do with soldiers, the armed forces, or war

promoting: trying to make something popular

quotes: repeats a person or piece of writing word for word

terrorize: to frighten someone a great deal

translated: made understandable

Venetians: people from Venice

Index

Photo Credits